IMAGES
of America

CLEVELAND IN
WORLD WAR I

IMAGES
of America

CLEVELAND IN
WORLD WAR I

Dale Thomas

ARCADIA
PUBLISHING

Published by Arcadia Publishing
Charleston, South Carolina

Printed in the United States of America

Library of Congress Control Number: 2015960068

For all general information, please contact Arcadia Publishing:
Telephone 843-853-2070
Fax 843-853-0044
E-mail sales@arcadiapublishing.com
For customer service and orders:
Toll-Free 1-888-313-2665

Visit us on the Internet at www.arcadiapublishing.com

For my wife, Lea Thomas, and our sons, Geoffrey and Scot

CONTENTS

ACKNOWLEDGMENTS

Lea Thomas proofread the text and offered suggestions. Geoffrey and Scot Thomas helped with computer hardware and software issues. The following provided additional assistance: Jennifer Nieves at the Dittrick Medical History Center, Case Western Reserve University; Alicia Naab at the Cleveland Public Library; William Stark at Grays Armory; Nancy Gillahan at the Berea Historical Society; Gary Porter at the Olmsted Historical Society; Georgia Beavis of Berea, Ohio; and Margaret Thomas of Painesville, Ohio.

The images in this book appear through the courtesy of Berea Historical Society (BHS); Cleveland Public Library (CPL); Dittrick Medical History Center, Case Western Reserve University (DMHC, CWRU); *International Socialist Review* magazine (ISRM); Library of Congress (LC); Local Cleveland Socialist Party (LCSP); National Archives (NA); National Library of Medicine (NLM); and Olmsted Historical Society (OHS).

INTRODUCTION

America entered World War I on April 6, 1917, after Germany resumed unrestrictive submarine warfare. Cleveland's contribution to victory over the Central Powers included the role of its prominent citizens. Newton D. Baker, former mayor of the city, served as Pres. Woodrow Wilson's secretary of war. Formerly in charge of Cleveland's Civil Service Commission, Benedict Crowell became Baker's assistant in the War Department. A son of Pres. James A. Garfield, Harry A. Garfield supervised the Federal Fuel Administration. Dr. George W. Crile headed a team of physicians and nurses from Cleveland's Lakeside Hospital that went to France. After serving as ambassador to France, Myron T. Herrick returned to Cleveland and later became chairman of the Mayor's Advisory War Committee. Charles W. Chesnutt, an African American author and civil rights leader, worked on the same committee, which dealt with local issues brought on by the war.

Cleveland's home front, however, included others who opposed the war. As a Socialist, Charles E. Ruthenberg spoke at a Cleveland rally criticizing the draft. Tried and found guilty of violating the Espionage Act of 1917, Ruthenberg spent the last year of the war in prison. Socialist candidate for president Eugene V. Debs defied the Sedition Act of 1918 in a speech given in Canton, Ohio, which led to a federal trial in Cleveland and a sentence of 10 years in prison. After Armistice Day, a Red Scare swept Cleveland and the rest of the country in 1919.

Cleveland's contribution to the war front began on May 25, 1917, with the Lakeside Hospital Unit becoming the first American detachment to land in Europe. On the home front, the war accelerated the growth of Cleveland, which would become the fifth-largest city in the nation by the end of the decade.

Wartime legislation passed in Washington profoundly affected Cleveland and the rest of the nation. The War Industries Board, Fuel Administration, and Food Administration utilized measures to regulate the economy in order to deal with shortages. The Committee on Public Information used the media to encourage support for the war.

When war broke out, Cleveland's growing industries could no longer depend on the labor emigrating from Europe. At the same time, 40,000 Clevelanders would eventually leave the workforce and serve in the military. Women replaced them in jobs never available in the past. Seeking employment, African Americans left the South, and this Great Migration led to significant economic, social, and political developments in the coming years.

Cleveland's ethnic neighborhoods included many who had come from the nations and regions of the Central Powers. Americanization programs taught the immigrants English and patriotism. Czechs, Slovaks, and Poles supported the war against their ancestral homelands, which they hoped would become independent after the war. Until the czar's abdication, Jews were generally reluctant to support the Allies because of the pogroms in Russia. Zionists looked forward to the creation of Israel after the Allies' victory in the Near East. The founding of Israel occurred after World War II.

In January 1918, a winter storm paralyzed Cleveland and the Middle West for a number of days. Due to the priority of war production, coal shortages made the subzero temperatures even harder to endure. An influenza epidemic struck later in the year, disrupting the home front. Armistice Day ended the war in November, but the disease continued to wreak havoc into the new year.

Cleveland suburb Berea had more than its share of turmoil and tragedy. In December 1917, anti-German hysteria gripped the campus of Baldwin-Wallace College. Today, on Berea's Triangle, a memorial plaque continues to remind the casual pedestrian of the 226 residents from Berea and Middleburg Township who served in World War I. Stars mark the 13 on the list who died in the so-called War to End All Wars. American Legion Post 91 in Berea is named after Lt. Albert E. Baesel.

A British soldier tends the grave of a comrade killed in the Battle of Arras, fought from April 8 to May 16, 1917. Soldiers from Britain, Canada, Newfoundland, South Africa, New Zealand, and Australia attacked German fortifications near the French city. The British suffered almost 160,000 casualties and the Germans around 125,000 casualties. America had declared war on Germany two days before the start of the offensive but would not be able to send an army to France for more than a year. Cleveland's Lakeside Hospital Unit went to France in May 1917 and treated British and Commonwealth soldiers. In his poem "The General," Siegfried Sassoon echoes the mood of a British Tommy at this time: " 'Good morning, good morning,' the general said, / When we met him last week on the way to the line. / Now the soldiers he smiled at are most of 'em dead, / And we're cursing his staff for incompetent swine. / 'He's a cherry old card,' muttered Harry to Jack / As they slogged to Arras with rifle and pack." (LC.)

One

LAKESIDE HOSPITAL UNIT

At Lakeside Avenue and East Fourteenth Street, Lakeside Hospital started a training school for nurses in 1898. The Medical Department of Western Reserve University sent medical students there for training. Working with Dr. George W. Crile, chief of surgery at the hospital, Agatha C. Hodgins founded the School of Anesthesia in 1911 and later the American Association of Nurse Anesthetists. (CPL.)

American ambassador to France Myron T. Herrick refused to leave Paris when the German offense threatened the city in August 1914. The Clevelander became a hero to the French people. During the crisis, Herrick assisted numerous compatriots seeking help at the American embassy. His greatest challenge was getting them safely out of France. (LC.)

After the French accepted his offer, Herrick got in touch with the State Department about the American Hospital of Paris treating wounded soldiers. The hospital began receiving casualties on September 7, 1914. Herrick contacted Dr. George W. Crile and asked his Cleveland friend to draw up plans for a surgical group, which became the American Ambulance in Paris. (LC.)

Congress declared war on April 6, 1917. Two years earlier, Surgeon General W.C. Gorgas asked Dr. George W. Crile to submit a plan for the coordination of civilian hospitals to provide their personnel for military service in Europe. As a result, Dr. Crile helped to establish base hospitals, which would treat Allied troops in France from 1917 to 1919. (CPL.)

Helen Briggs, a resident of North Olmsted, Ohio, graduated from the Lakeside Hospital Nursing School before the war. She would soon become an operating room nurse at Base Hospital No. 4. A perfectionist, Dr. George W. Crile expected those around him to follow his example. For someone so young at 23 years of age, Briggs must have impressed him with her competence. (DMHC, CWRU.)

The US Army activated Harry C. Hanford and other Cleveland reservists on May 5, 1917. He joined the 155 enlisted men of the Lakeside Hospital Unit, along with the doctors and nurses under the command of Maj. Harry L. Gilchrist. Promoted to sergeant in June 1917 and transferred to the Chief Surgeon's Office, Hanford became a first lieutenant on April 11, 1918, and later head of the Sanitation Department. (CPL.)

Erie View Avenue on the left overlooks Union Depot. The Lakeside Unit left Cleveland for New York on May 6, 1917. In a drizzling rain, officers and nurses rode in closed automobiles to the station, while the enlisted men carried their luggage and marched past city hall and the county courthouse. At the train station, the Red Cross gave each nurse a corsage bouquet. The train steamed out of the depot at 4:00 p.m. (LC.)

On May 8, Helen Briggs and the Lakeside Unit sailed out of New York Harbor and into the dangerous waters of the Atlantic Ocean. A week later, a submarine alarm turned out to be only a scare. However, the anxious passengers saw floating debris from a ship sunk by the Germans. A scheduled rendezvous with an American destroyer calmed their jittery nerves. A day later, on May 18, they docked in Liverpool. (DMHC, CWRU.)

Helen Briggs mailed a photograph and a clipping from the *London Daily Mirror* to her family in North Olmsted. Along with the surgeons and nurses, Briggs waits to shake hands with King George and Queen Mary. After the audience with the royal family, the nurses went to Marlborough House for a reception given by Queen Mother Alexandra. The following day, they rejoined their unit and left Southampton for France. (DMHC, CWRU.)

The Lakeside Unit disembarked at Rouen on the Seine River. Buses transported the personnel five miles to General Hospital No. 9 in the British sector of the western front since American troops had yet to arrive in France. The US Army Base Hospital No. 4 (Lakeside Unit) would ultimately treat 82,179 soldiers, most of them from Great Britain and the British Commonwealth. (DMHC, CWRU.)

Casualty Clearing Stations were located near the trenches, where the wounded and gassed received their initial treatment. Many died before being transported to the base hospitals. On July 17, 1917, nine ambulances carried the teams of doctors and nurses into Belgium. Helen Briggs and Dr. George W. Crile rode in Ambulance No. 8, loaded with supplies and two days of rations. German artillery and airplanes were a constant threat to these stations. (DMHC, CWRU.)

Helen Briggs served at the clearing station from July 17 to September 28. After the war, she received the British Royal Red Cross "for splendid Theatre work under trying conditions with a cheerfulness which creates a proper working atmosphere," as well as for "valuable work with a Surgical Team in a Front Area." The matron-in-chief of the British Forces had recommended her to Field Marshal Sir Douglas Haig. Winston Churchill, secretary of state for war, signed the citation. (DMHC, CWRU.)

Cassie Salisbury of North Olmsted (right), 10 years older than Helen Briggs, graduated from the Lakeside Hospital Nursing School in 1909. In September 1917, her ship was approaching the English coast when an underwater explosion made it tremble. The alarm sounded for them to stand by the lifeboats. However, the explosion was not a torpedo but a destroyer's depth charge blowing up a German submarine. Soon afterward, Salisbury joined the Lakeside Unit. (DMHC, CWRU.)

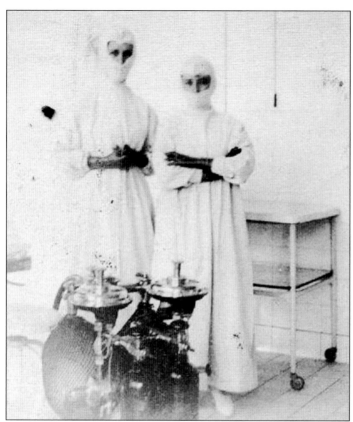

Cassie Salisbury (left) and Helen Briggs pose for this photograph just before the Germans would launch their Spring Offensive of 1918. Overwhelmed with the wounded soldiers, doctors operated day and night. On Easter Sunday, Dr. George W. Crile recorded more than 1,000 wounded soldiers arriving for treatment—the most ever for a single day. The British halted the attack at Cantigny on April 4, only 65 miles from Rouen. Americans helped to stop the German advance on Paris in June. (DMHC, CWRU.)

Helen Briggs sent this postcard home to North Olmsted. Censorship prevented her from writing letters about the dead and dying soldiers. In his journal, Dr. George W. Crile writes, "The seriously wounded piled up so fast that nothing could be done with them, so I told the Sister [nurse] to administer as near an overdose of morphine as was possible to keep them alive but free from suffering." (DMHC, CWRU.)

The Germans' final offensive of the war lasted from July 15 to August 6, 1918. As it was fought well beyond its sector, the Lakeside Unit did not receive casualties from this very costly battle, allowing the staff to take leaves. Helen Briggs (left) and Cassie Salisbury (right) went to the French Alps for a well-deserved vacation. They stayed at the Grand Hotel in Chamonix-Mont-Blanc, a ski resort. (DMHC, CWRU.)

After Armistice Day on November 11, 1918, the base hospitals mostly handled convalescents, and Helen Briggs had more free time. She spent many hours with a Captain G., who often took her to dinner in Rouen. She had written "Oo la la!" in her diary when he first asked for a date. Two weeks later, she received a Valentine from Ruben Elliott, serving with the 37th Division in France. They had attended the same high school. (DMHC, CWRU.)

The nurses went to Brest and anxiously awaited the voyage home. Helen Briggs hoped to see Ruben Elliott, who she heard was also awaiting passage to America. She telephoned him and they met. Briggs writes in her diary, "We sat on the bank and talked. I wonder when I'll see him next and what will happen." The nurses left France in March 1919. After docking in New Jersey, they took the train to Cleveland, arriving home on April 9. (LC.)

Helen Briggs married Reuben Elliott in 1919. In the 1930s, they purchased this house built by her ancestor in 1836. Helen died of leukemia at the age of 48, most likely from exposure to the radiation from hundreds of X-rays taken of wounded soldiers. In 1969, the Olmsted Historical Society moved the original part of the house to Frostville in the Rocky River Reservation of the Cleveland Metroparks. (OHS.)

Two

BUCKEYE DIVISION

A production of *Everyman* drew large crowds to Grays Armory in October 1903. Impresario Carl Frohman, a native Ohioan, had brought the morality play to America from England. He died while traveling on the *Lusitania* in May 1915. Headquartered at the armory, the Cleveland Grays militia formed the nucleus of the 37th "Buckeye" Division's 148th Regiment in 1917. (LC.)

Charles B. Winder, a colonel in the Ohio National Guard, won a gold medal in the team rifle competition at the London Olympic Games in 1908. He had enlisted in the guard at the age of 23 in 1897 and served during the Spanish-American War. Working with Winchester, he helped develop the Winder Musket, a single-shot rifle used in shooting events. During World War I, Winder served in Army Ordnance. (LC.)

In March 1909, the Ohio National Guardsmen await their departure for home. They had come to Washington, DC, for the inauguration of fellow Ohioan William H. Taft. Because of a winter storm, the swearing-in ceremony took place within the Capitol. A brigade of 6,000 workers spent half the night clearing the parade route. (LC.)

After war broke out in Europe, Frank A. Scott, a Cleveland business executive, campaigned for military preparedness. He became a member of the US Naval Consulting Board in 1916 and then chair of the Munitions Standards Board when America entered the war. However, Scott resigned within the year because of poor health. Scott later became treasurer and vice president of Lakeside Hospital. (LC.)

In March 1916, Brig. Gen. John J. Pershing led regular army troops into Mexico, searching for Pancho Villa, who had raided Columbus, New Mexico. Pres. Woodrow Wilson and War Secretary Newton D. Baker watch the National Guard parading in Washington before departing to the New Mexico border in June 1916. (LC.)

The Ohio National Guard left the Mexican border earlier than expected because of the growing submarine crisis with Germany. In the years leading up to America entering the war in Europe, preparedness had become a national slogan for meeting the threat of German militarism. College and high school students learned the basics of soldiering to prepare them for training in the National Guard or the Army. (LC.)

Prepared or not, the nation went to war on April 6, 1917. After announcing unrestricted submarine warfare, Germany correctly gambled that the US Army would not be a major factor on the western front for at least a year. The War Department ordered the mobilization of National Guard soldiers in May. Cleveland's Central Armory became the headquarters of the assembling militia, which numbered more than 1,000 men of the Fifth Ohio National Guard. (CPL.)

Creel Committee posters did not always need propaganda to make a point. Many young men were eager to join the National Guard once the nation went to war. However, some might have hesitated until seeing friends and neighbors head for the recruiting office. They were "getting on the bandwagon" and not being left behind. (LC.)

John R. Southam joined the Fifth Ohio National Guard while still a student at Berea High School. He went on to attend Baldwin University and later built houses in Cleveland's West Park neighborhood. Captain Southam commanded troops on the Mexican border. Shortly after his return to Cleveland, Southam became a major in the Fifth Ohio National Guard, later the 145th Infantry of the 37th "Buckeye" Division. (OHS.)

Capt. John Blossom was born in Cleveland in May 1891. He served in Headquarters Company of the 147th Infantry, 37th Division. On October 25, 1917, the War Department combined three Ohio National Guard regiments to form the 147th Infantry Regiment at Camp Sheridan, Alabama. After the war, Blossom, a stockbroker, lived in Shaker Heights, Ohio. (CPL.)

George Ruple (left) and Ruben W. Elliott (right) lived in North Olmsted. Elliott attended the Case School of Applied Science and graduated with a degree in mechanical engineering. At Central Armory on July 18, 1917, he enlisted in the First Ohio Engineers, which became the 112th Engineer Regiment of the 37th Division. Elliott would become a master of engineers senior grade by November 23, 1917. After the war, he married Helen Briggs. (Courtesy of Nancy Mitchell.)

George Creel believed his job was to sell the war to the public as though it were a product advertised for purchase and consumption. At the same time, he realized patriotism had to be supplemented by the ambitions of prospective enlistees. Unlike Ruben Elliott, most had not graduated from college and wanted to learn a trade while also serving their country. (LC.)

The Gordon Park pavilion overlooks the beach and lake near the site of the engineer camp. Col. J.R. McQuigg denied a rumor that immoral women had been in and around the camp. He said women have to apply at his headquarters for permission to enter the camp, and they are usually mothers, wives, and sisters. (LC.)

At Gordon Park on August 10, 1917, Ruben Elliott trained with the 1st Engineer Regiment of the Ohio National Guard, soon to be mobilized as the 112th Engineer Regiment in the National Army. On the left, the statue of Commodore Oliver Hazard Perry (War of 1812) looks down on the soldiers of yet another war. Rope fences and Keep Out signs kept intruders out of the former picnic grounds. According to a *Plain Dealer* reporter, "A long array of white tents, set up in orderly

rows, impresses the visitor that this is serious business afoot and that this erstwhile picnic grounds now serves a sterner purpose . . . From the lake clear back to the tennis courts, the space is filled with these earnest young soldiers of tomorrow setting about light heartedly on this 'big adventure,' the end of which no man knows." (LC.)

On the west side of Cleveland, three companies of the Sixth Ohio National Guard Infantry encamped at Edgewater Park. Many of them friends and relatives, a crowd showed up as if this were a typical Sunday band concert. They saw the Guardsmen march and then break ranks for inspection of their tents. The festive atmosphere ignored the grim days ahead for these soldiers. (CPL.)

The Creel Committee employed artists who often used the symbolism of Uncle Sam and the American flag to encourage enlistments. A true patriot would not wait for the draft. Secretary of State Robert Lansing, War Secretary Newton D. Baker, and Navy Secretary Josephus Daniels were ex officio members of the Committee for Public Information. (LC.)

In July 1917, the Machine Gun Company of the Fifth Ohio National Guard (145th Infantry, 37th Division) took up residence in Grays Armory. Capt. Charles C. Chambers (first row, center) conducted drills besides lecturing on military tactics. He allowed those who lived locally to leave at the end of the day. In his book *Heaven, Hell, or Hoboken*, Pvt. Ray N. Johnson remembers the two months there as a time of innocence for the soldiers, who had little to no knowledge of what to expect in the future. After the morning roll call in front of the armory, the men marched to "Payne's Pasture for two hours of drill," according to Johnson, who goes on to say, "We were allowed to fall out to rest and smoke about every ten minutes." Afterward, they marched back on Euclid Avenue and then East Fourteenth Street while singing "The Machine Gun Men" and "The Jackass Battery." Usually, they were off duty after lunch. (Ohio National Guard.)

The Fifth Ohio National Guard assembled outside of Central Armory on September 25, 1917. Soon to be renamed the 145th Regiment of the 37th "Buckeye" Division, the unit included soldiers from Cleveland, Berea, Elyria, Warren, Painesville, Ashtabula, and Norwalk. Here, they march south on East Sixth Street as the crowd cheers at the intersection of Superior Avenue. The parade continued onto Euclid Avenue and then to Public Square. (CPL.)

Approaching Union Depot at the foot of West Sixth Street, the crowd surged around the soldiers, and some had to break ranks. The *Plain Dealer* summarizes the day as follows: "Cleveland bids the Fifth [National Guard] goodbye regretfully but proudly. Its officers have been so long with us and its ranks are composed of men taken from local industries. They marched with the steadiness of real soldiers, confident of their power." (LC.)

PRIVILEGE *means* RESPONSIBILITY

Out on Time   Back on Time

At Camp Sheridan in Alabama, the 145th Regiment spent sixteen weeks of basic training, then advanced training in the trenches of the infantry, artillery, and machine gun ranges. After the denial of Christmas furloughs, the Buckeyes were surprised when Gov. James M. Cox of Ohio reviewed the 37th Division on December 24, 1917. He had come to the camp on a train loaded with gifts from Ohioans. While on leave, the Buckeyes usually went to Montgomery, four miles from Camp Sheridan. Most of them saw for the first time the ubiquitous segregation of African Americans. Two hotels, the Gay Teague and Exchange, became the meeting and gathering places for the soldiers. Until running out of money, the men enjoyed the theaters, ice-cream parlors, and pool halls. Buses usually took them to Montgomery, but they either walked or took a taxi back to the base. (LC.)

On October 19, 1917, Albert Baesel of Berea sent a postcard from his station at Camp Sheridan to his parents. It includes the following message: "Hello Folks, I got your letter and expect you to write again soon. Things are getting better all the time here and the weather is fine. Expect to get some drafted men soon." Commissioned a second lieutenant the following May, he transferred from the 145th Regiment to the 148th Regiment of the 37th Division. (BHS.)

Maj. Gen. Charles S. Farnsworth assumed command of the 37th Division in May 1918 as the Buckeyes transferred to Camp Lee at Petersburg, Virginia. The division left for Europe by way of Hoboken, New Jersey, on June 12 and arrived in France 10 days later. The men journeyed on the USS *Leviathan*, formerly the *Vaterland*, a German liner seized by the American government. (LC.)

The 37th Division fought in the Lorraine, Ypres-Lys, and Meuse-Argonne Campaigns. After the war, Lucien Jonas drew his depiction of the Meuse-Argonne Campaign, which began on September 26 and ended with Armistice Day on November 11, 1918. More than a million American soldiers saw action in the bloodiest battle in the nation's history. Among the more than 120,000 casualties, 26,000 soldiers died. (LC.)

HIS LIBERTY BOND

PAID FOR IN FULL

W.A. Rogers drew this poignant picture of a dead soldier who could have been someone's son, brother, or husband. In the Machine Gun Company of the 145th Infantry Regiment, eight were killed in action, three died of wounds, and two died from disease. In addition, the casualties included 28 wounded and six gassed. (LC.)

In Columbus, Ohio, the statue of a doughboy honors the 37th Division fighting with the American Expeditionary Forces. His grim expression mirrors the 5,387 casualties, including the 1,348 soldiers who died in World War I. Ohio State University instructor Bruce Saville sculpted the nine-foot-tall *Victorious Soldier* in 1926. Martin P. Coady served as Saville's model. Coady was a veteran of the division and an architecture student at the university. Originally, the statue stood at North High Street and Fifteenth Avenue on the university's campus. With the relocation of the Ohio Historical Society in 1970, the doughboy found a new home for a few years on the auditorium's roof and was then later stored in a garage. After restoration in 1991, the statue now stands in front of the Ohio Historical Society. Today, the Reserve Officers's Training Corps at Ohio State University continues the tradition of the Buckeyes' service to the US Army. (Author's collection.)

Three

CONSCRIPTION AND ENLISTMENT

A progressive Democrat in Cleveland, Newton D. Baker served as city solicitor and then mayor from 1912 to 1915. He knew Woodrow Wilson from his time at Johns Hopkins University. Baker worked for Wilson's presidential nomination in 1912 and some delegates saw him as a possible running mate. President Wilson appointed Baker as secretary of war in 1916, making him the youngest member of his cabinet. (LC.)

In Washington, DC, War Secretary Newton D. Baker stood blindfolded next to a glass jar containing 10,500 capsules on July 20, 1917. He reached in and drew the first number. A clerk opened the capsule and announced No. 258, which represented 4,557 men who had registered for the draft in June. After Baker removed the blindfold, the drawing continued with those designated for duty in charge. The lottery took 15 hours to determine the order of induction for the 9,659,382 registrants. The Army would select 687,000 for the first draft. A week later in Cleveland, the first summonses notified 4,730 of 8,183 men in Cuyahoga County to report for physical examinations on the third floor of the new county courthouse. With a serial number of 258 in District 15, Sven Hansen of 1420 East Eighty-Fourth Street was first on the list. Eventually, examinations for the rest of the quota also took place at city and suburban schools. (LC.)

Arthur C. Berry registered for the draft in Urbana, Ohio, on June 5, 1917. He had served with the Ohio National Guard and held the rank of a noncommissioned officer. At 30 years old, Berry asked for a deferment because of a physical disability. Before returning to his hometown, he had worked in Cleveland as a county bookkeeper and lived in a boardinghouse on Prospect Avenue. (OHS.)

In April 1918, Berry received notification in the mail of his induction into the US Army: "Failure to report promptly at the hour and day named is a grave military offense for which you may be court-martialed. Willful failure to report with an intent to evade military service constitutes desertion from the Army of the United States, which, in time of war is a capital offense." (LC.)

CAMP SHERMAN, CHILLICOTHE, OHIO.

Berry and the other draftees went by train to Camp Sherman, Ohio, and took basic training with the 330th Infantry. In June 1918, the regiment went to France with the 83rd Division, which became a depot division in the Fourth Army Corps. After becoming a corporal, Berry worked in a supply company of the 331st Infantry and never saw combat. (LC.)

Alfonso Proctor (right) was drafted while living in Barberton, Ohio. He served in the 59th Infantry and occasionally enjoyed a glass of wine with Berry in a nearby town. Soon after this picture was taken, Proctor's regiment went to the front and he suffered a serious wound while fighting in the Meuse-Argonne Campaign. On June 4, 1919, he received an honorable discharge with a 25 percent disability. (OHS.)

On August 30, 1918, Berry mailed a postcard to his future wife, Isabelle Cattrell, a clerk at the Cleveland Trust Bank: "Received my first letter from Mother about two days ago and none since not even from you. Two weeks seems a long while not to get any letters to us boys over here. Hope you are well and happy, remember me to everybody. With much love, Arthur." (OHS.)

The Cleveland Trust Bank, the second building from the left, stands on the corner of Euclid Avenue and East Ninth Street. All of Berry's letters to Cattrell were addressed to her at the bank. On November 14, 1918, Berry sent another postcard: "My dear Isabelle, hurrah the war is over. Everybody is happy but the Germans and to hell with him." He spent the postwar years working for the bank. (CPL.)

The Creel Committee employed Howard Chandler Christy, among other artists. On the surface, his poster comes across as amusing, but it infers that if a man does not enlist, then he is a coward. The techniques of propaganda include getting on the bandwagon and glittering generalities. Nearly 13,000 women did join the Navy and Marines. (LC.)

Johnny Kilbane (left) held the featherweight championship for more than 11 years. He grew up in the Angle, an Irish neighborhood on Cleveland's Near West Side. After defeating Abe Attell for the title, Kilbane returned to his hometown on St. Patrick's Day of 1912. Mayor Newton D. Baker broke a rule against official appearances on Sunday and reviewed the parade from a stand in front of city hall. (CPL.)

Johnny Kilbane entered the Army on October 15, 1917, not as a draftee or enlistee, but as an employee. At Camp Sherman, Kilbane (left) poses with Capt. M. De Brissoc Owen, a bayonet instructor. Besides making public appearances for the Army, Kilbane served as boxing director and taught self-defense until November 30, 1918. (CPL.)

Lt. Arthur D. Baldwin, Hawaiian-born in 1876, enlisted on November 27, 1917, and served in the 164th Field Artillery Brigade. He took part in the fighting at Saint-Mihiel. Baldwin received an honorable discharge on May 31, 1919, and returned to practicing law in Cleveland. He lived with his family of seven, as well as five servants, on Lake Shore Boulevard in Bratenahl, Ohio. (CPL.)

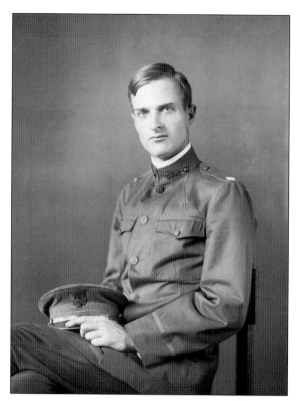

Charles Francis Brush Jr., son of the successful inventor and entrepreneur, enlisted in the US Army Ordnance on September 19, 1917. Before his discharge as a first lieutenant in January 1919, he spent time in Washington, DC; Syracuse, New York; and Sheffield, Alabama. After his son's death in 1927, Charles Francis Brush Sr. set up the Brush Foundation at the Western Reserve University Medical School. (CPL.)

In November 1917, Andrew T. Chisholm enlisted at the age of 37 and rose to the rank of captain in the 337th Infantry. His regiment spent nearly nine months in France, returning in April 1919. He was president of the Chisholm Steel Co. and lived on Euclid Avenue at East Ninetieth Street. (CPL.)

The Creel Committee appealed to young men seeking careers after the war. In addition, there was the romantic portrayal of combat to lure them into enlisting. "Give 'er the gun" of course ignored the notion of the enemy shooting back. Slogans or catchphrases, however, appealed to a person's expectation of adventure and glory while fighting for one's country. (LC.)

Louise and Henning Larson pose for this photograph in 1919. A Clevelander of Swedish ancestry, Henning enlisted on October 3, 1917, and took basic training at Camp Sherman. In February 1918, he went to France, serving as a chauffeur in Headquarters Company of the First Air Service Mechanics Regiment. His unit trained with the French army until July 5, 1918. Maj. Charles Livingston promoted him to chauffeur first class in December 1918. (Courtesy of Norm and Chris Rehark.)

Lucius J. Clay lived on East 100th Street in Cleveland when he enlisted in December 1917. After basic training at Fort Wayne in Michigan, he attended the School of Military Aeronautics at Cornell University. Lieutenant Clay spent time at Dorr Field in Florida and Barron Field in Texas. Discharged in January 1919, he lived in Shreveport, Louisiana, where he worked as an oil lease broker. (CPL.)

Lt. Charles E. Dangler received his commission at Fort Benjamin Harrison in Indianapolis, Indiana, in August 1917. He went to France with the 329th Infantry, a regiment in the 83rd Division. Dangler returned to Cleveland in February 1919 and became an office clerk for a scrap iron company. He later operated his own filling station and lived in Shaker Heights. (CPL.)

Lt. Fred H. Emery spent most of his army time with the 349th Infantry in the 92nd Division. He left Camp Dix, New Jersey, for France in June 1918 and served in the Defensive Sector for the next nine months. After his discharge, Emery returned to Cleveland Heights and his stockbroker job. He later moved to Aurora, Ohio. (CPL.)

Henry B. Fuller was a sergeant in the signal corps of the 49th Aero Squadron. The US Army Air Service patch is seen on his shoulder. He entered the Army in March 1918 and did not join the unit in France until that October. In three months, the squadron's SPAD pursuit planes shot down 24 German aircraft. After the war, Fuller lived with his widowed mother in Cleveland and worked in a management position at a steel company. (CPL.)

Before activation from the Army Reserves, Capt. Benjamin P. Bole poses with his son Patrick. He briefly served on the Mayor's Advisory War Committee, then left for Fort Benjamin Harrison, Indiana, in August 1917. Promoted to major, Bole saw action in the Meuse-Argonne Campaign. His honorable discharge occurred on May 12, 1919. (CPL.)

Three grandsons of Pres. James A. Garfield enlisted in the Army: (from left to right) Capt. John Garfield served in the 134th Field Artillery in the Meuse-Argonne Campaign, Maj. Newell Garfield saw action in the same campaign as a member of the 322nd Field Artillery, and, unlike his cousins, Maj. James Garfield spent the war teaching in the field artillery school at Fort Sill, Oklahoma. President Wilson appointed his father to head the Fuel Administration. (CPL.)

Capt. Horace K. Havlicek of Cleveland served in a cadet regiment before graduating from Ohio State University in 1916. At the age of 21, Havlicek joined the 6th Cavalry of the 2nd Division in 1917. While training at Fort Sam Houston in Texas, he died from a gunshot wound suffered on a firing range. (BHS.)

While attending Yale University in 1916, David S. Ingalls of Cleveland might have seen this exhibition, which motivated him to enlist in the Naval Reserve Flying Corps. Activated for duty in April 1917, he trained and received his pilot license and commission to lieutenant before assignment to the Royal Air Force in England. Ingalls flew for RAF Squadron 213 and shot down six German aircraft. (LC.)

Commodore Frederick Ceres (left) and David S. Ingalls shake hands in 1929. After the war, Ingalls graduated from Harvard Law School in 1923 and joined Squire, Sanders & Dempsey in Cleveland. He left the law firm and served in the Ohio Legislature in 1927. Pres. Herbert Hoover selected him as assistant secretary of the Navy for aeronautics in 1929. His agenda included the strengthening of the Navy's carrier aircraft fleet. He ran unsuccessfully for governor of Ohio in 1932, and Mayor Harry L. Davis appointed him Cleveland welfare director. Nevertheless, Ingalls resigned in 1935 when the mayor declined to install X-ray machines in City Hospital. During World War II, Ingalls became a rear admiral and served as chief of staff for the Pacific Forward Area Air Center Command. For his service, he received the Bronze Star and the Legion of Merit medals. The National Aviation Hall of Fame made him a member in 1983. (LC.)

Four

MAYOR'S WAR COMMITTEE

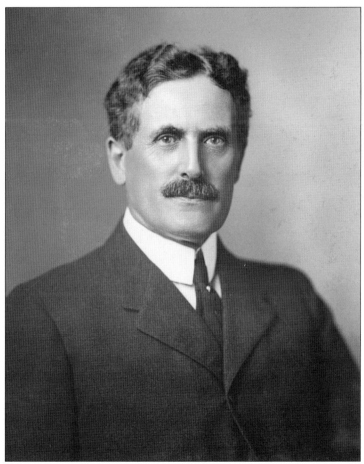

Mayor Harry L. Davis created the Mayor's Advisory War Committee on April 7, 1917. He appointed nearly 70 members of the community, including business, civic, and religious leaders. Davis selected Myron T. Herrick (pictured), a banker and former ambassador to France, as the chair of the committee. For the duration of the war, Herrick would take part in a number of local programs. He posed for this photograph while ambassador to France. (CPL.)

A corporate lawyer and president of Cleveland Trust Bank, Frederick H. Goff became the treasurer of the committee. He had been mayor of Glenville before its annexation to Cleveland. Goff helped to establish the Cleveland Foundation. President Wilson later appointed him to the War Finance Corporation, where he worked as vice chair of the Capital Issues Committee. (CPL.)

President of the Cleveland Chamber of Commerce Paul L. Feiss served on the Executive Committee. He helped to coordinate a number of projects, including soldiers' welfare, war gardens, community festivals, women's activities, housing regulations, bond drives, speakers' bureau, draft board supervision, fundraising, and Americanization. He also represented Cleveland for the Division of Housing of the Department of Labor. (CPL.)

Author and humanitarian Charles W. Chesnutt represented African Americans on the Mayor's Advisory War Committee. His parents were freed slaves living in Cleveland at the time of his birth in 1858. With Booker T. Washington and W.E.B. Du Bois, Chesnutt served on the General Committee of the National Association for the Advancement of Colored People. (CPL.)

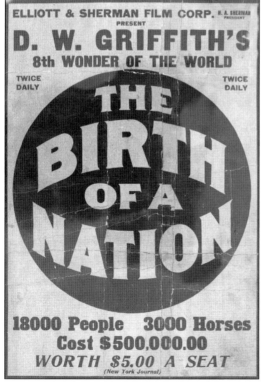

On February 7, 1917, Chesnutt and a party of African Americans went to see Mayor Davis to protest the showing of *The Birth of a Nation*. "I do not know at this time whether we have the power to bar the picture," he told a *Plain Dealer* reporter, "but I don't think it ought to be shown. A picture that might tend to create race prejudice should not be exhibited." (LC.)

Sow the seeds of Victory!

plant & raise your own vegetables

WRITE TO THE NATIONAL WAR GARDEN COMMISSION — WASHINGTON, D.C. for free books on gardening, canning & drying.

"Every Garden a Munition Plant"

Charles Lathrop Pack, President

Miss Liberty shows the way for patriotic Americans to follow. The Mayor's Advisory War Committee promoted the planting of war gardens to increase the nation's food supply during the war. Clevelanders could write to the National War Garden Commission in Washington to receive free books about gardening, canning, and drying produce. (LC.)

With his wife and two daughters, Charles W. Chesnutt lived at 9719 Lamont Avenue near East 100th Street in Cleveland. The Chesnutts had a large backyard with flower gardens. In the book about her father, *Chesnutt, Pioneer of the Color Line*, Helen M. Chesnutt writes, "During the spring and summer [1918], the entire family labored faithfully in their war garden, which was extensive." (CPL.)

The Woman's Subcommittee of the War Committee divided the city into zones for neighborhood meetings. Members taught classes on the gardening, canning, and drying of vegetables. Food conservation was another topic on the agenda. As suggested by the poster, those attending these classes were doing their part to "Can the Kaiser" and win the war. (LC.)

The architectural firm of Hubbell & Benes designed a new West Side Market building, which opened to merchants and shoppers in 1912. The interior concourse had a hundred stalls and an exterior arcade accommodated 85 stands. The clock tower quickly became a landmark for the neighborhood. War gardens soon increased the produce for sale. (CPL.)

The Sheriff Street Market on East Fourth Street and Huron Avenue sold vegetables from the war gardens on the east side of Cleveland. During the growing season of 1918, gardeners in the city harvested enough fresh vegetables to feed the entire US Army for 10 weeks. Churches and factories cultivated community gardens. (LC.)

Under Herbert Hoover in Washington, the US Food Administration requested the help of the War Committee to provide assistance in its national campaign to eliminate wasted food. The committee erected this sign on the Public Square in Cleveland: "Eat less wheat, beef, pork, fats, and sugar." In addition, the committee created a local food board to administrate the program, which included the fining of hoarders and price gougers. (LC.)

Former health commissioner of Cleveland Dr. R.H. Bishop Jr. supervised the work of the food board, which distributed posters to bakery and grocery stores in the city. The weekly consumption of flour fell by one third. At the same time, Clevelanders saved an estimated million and a half pounds of sugar a month. (LC.)

Save a loaf
a week
help win
the war

U.S. FOOD ADMINISTRATION

The Diebolt Brewing Company stable for beer wagon horses once stood on Pittsburgh Avenue and East Twenty-Seventh Street. A total of 26 breweries operated in Cleveland in 1910. Once America entered the war, anti-German propaganda began associating beer with Germany. The Anti-Saloon League eventually shut down the industry. Only Pilsener, Standard, Forest City, and Cleveland Home Brewing reopened after Prohibition. (LC.)

In 1913, the Anti-Saloon League held its annual convention in Columbus, Ohio, the home and birthplace of the association. World War I hastened the victory of the Prohibitionists in the state and the nation. Besides alcohol causing social problems, they argued, the ingredients in the brewing of beer and the distilling of whiskey added to the shortage of food. After a close defeat in 1917, the league won a referendum in 1918 making Ohio a dry state. (LC.)

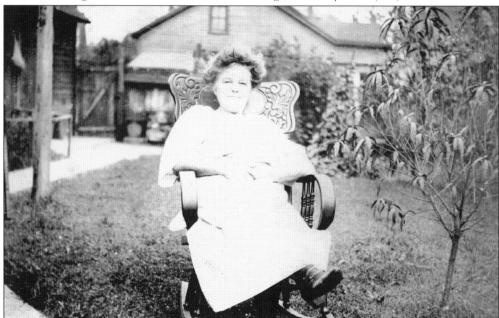

Marie Kmetz came to America from Slovakia, then a region in Austria-Hungary. She married Michael Zakutna, another Slovak immigrant, who died in 1906. During the war, her brother was drafted into the Hungarian army. Prohibition tended to be unpopular among Slovaks and other Eastern European immigrants. In Cleveland's Broadway community, Marie operated a still in her home and sold the liquor to neighbors. Unlike her four children, she never learned to speak English. (Author's Collection.)

On March 5, 1918, the *Plain Dealer* quoted Samuel Hopkins Adams, who praised Mayor Davis for the Americanization program: "Cleveland woke up one morning after war was declared to find that three-fourths of its population was of foreign birth or parentage . . . The city is holding out to the alien within its gates the hand not of condescending assistance, but the fellowship of the United States of America." (LC.)

TO ALL ALIENS

IF the WAR has affected your LIVING or WORKING conditions,

IF you WANT to learn the AMERICAN LANGUAGE and become a CITIZEN,

IF you WISH Employment, Advice or Information,

Without Charge,

Apply to—

Room 1820, MUNICIPAL BUILDING
MAYOR'S COMMITTEE ON NATIONAL DEFENSE
COMMITTEE on ALIENS.

AN SÄMTLICHE NICHT NATURALISIERTEN AUSLÄNDER:

Diejenigen, deren EXISTENZBEDINGUNGEN oder ARBEITSVERHÄLT-NISSEinfolge des KRIEGES geschädigt sind,

Die die AMERIKANISCHE SPRACHE zu erlernen und das BÜRGER-RECHTzu erwerben wünschen,

Die BESCHÄFTIGUNG finden oder RAT bezw. AUSKUNFT einholen möchten, und zwar kostenfrei, sind aufgefordert, sich zu melden im

MUNIZIPALGEBÄUDE, Zimmer 1820
Die vom Bürgermeister eingesetzte Landesvertheidigungs-Kommission
Ausschuss für nicht-naturalisierte Ausländer.

Minden külföldi szülöttnek.

Ha a háboru hatást gyakorolt életmódjára vagy munka viszonyaira,

Ha kívánja megtanulni az amerikai nyelvet és megszerezni a polgári jogot,

Ha foglalkoz ást, tanácsot vagy felvilágosítást kíván

díjmentesen,

Forduljon a

Városház 1820 számu szobájában lévő
Polgármester nemzeti védelem bizottságához
Külföldiek bizottságához.

Všetkým v cudzozemsku narodeným.

Keď vojna mala účinok na spôsob vášho žitia alebo na vaše pracovné pomery,

Keď sa chcete naučiť americkú reč a stať sa občanom,

Keď chcete dostať prácu, poradu alebo vysvetlenie

bez poplatku,

Obráťte sa na

Izbu číslo 1820, v mestkom dome
Mayorov Výbor Národnej Obrany
Výbor Cudzozemcov.

After graduating from Baldwin University in 1906, Raymond Moley taught at the Kennedy Ridge School near Columbia Road in North Olmsted, among other schools in Berea and Olmsted Falls. He received a master of arts from Oberlin College in 1913 and a doctorate from Columbia University in 1918. In the meantime, Moley taught political science at Western Reserve University and chaired the Americanization Board in Cleveland. In January 1932, he formed FDR's Brain Trust. (LC.)

With the assistance of Raymond Moley, Eleanor Edwards Ledbetter wrote three books for the War Committee to encourage the Americanization of Czechs, Slovaks, and Yugoslavs. As librarian for Cleveland's Broadway Branch, she supervised English language and citizenship classes, which influenced other branches, as pictured at the Woodland Library. After the war, Czechoslovakia honored Ledbetter for her work in aiding its emigrants. (CPL.)

Americanization through the buying of bonds was the goal of this poster: teach the immigrants English but at the same time give them a stake in a victory over the Central Powers. They came to this country seeking liberty, and now the time had come to help America in this struggle against tyranny. (LC.)

On May 3, 1918, Cleveland held a third Liberty bond campaign in tents on the Public Square. As president of the American Federation of Labor, Samuel Gompers spoke about labor unions backing of the war. Douglas Fairbanks represented the support of Hollywood. Former world heavyweight boxing champion "Gentleman Jim" Corbett gave a short talk on patriotism. (CPL.)

The War Committee enhanced the Labor Day parade of 1917 with a more patriotic theme to the traditional event. Marching from the Public Square on Superior Avenue, trade unions carried American flags besides their own banners. In June 1918, a subcommittee organized a Flag Day celebration in Wade Park, which drew thousands of people. (CPL.)

The Great Lakes Navy Band came to Cleveland in 1918 and paraded on Superior Avenue. The War Committee supported the visit, which coincided with campaigns to increase bond sales and naval recruitment. Visitors from abroad included the French Foreign Legion and British airmen. Mayor Davis welcomed them and utilized his committee to arrange accommodations and events. (CPL.)

HOME HOSPITALITY

The Spirit of

WAR CAMP
COMMUNITY SERVICE
UNITED WAR WORK CAMPAIGN

WAR CAMP COMMUNITY SERVICE

The War Camp Community Service, a national organization, promoted social relationships between civilians and military personnel. The War Committee encouraged Clevelanders to show hospitality toward soldiers and sailors who were temporarily in the city. The Young Men's Christian Association and the Salvation Army also provided services to help the morale of these young men. (LC.)

Five

IMMIGRANTS AND MIGRANTS

Cleveland's diverse population gathered in the city's downtown market district. In the decade prior to World War I, 70 percent of the immigrants arriving in the United States came from Eastern and Southern Europe. The census of 1920 showed that 15 percent of the nation's population had been born in this region. African Americans from the South increased this urban diversification. (CPL.)

In a display of Americanization, Cleveland's Slovenian Division marched in the Perry Centennial Parade on September 17, 1913, celebrating the American victory over the British in the Battle of Lake Erie. At the time, nearly 30,000 Slovenes lived in the city, mostly in east side neighborhoods. They built the Slovenian National Home at 5409 St. Clair Avenue to accommodate their lodges

and associations. When America went to war, more than 400 Slovenes from Cleveland enlisted in the military. After centuries of Austrian domination, Slovenes, Croats, and Serbs formed Yugoslavia on October 29, 1918. Some Slovenes returned to their homeland, but an overwhelming number now saw themselves as Americans. (LC.)

With the outbreak of war in Europe, American Jews and Poles had little, if any, sympathy for Russia, the ally of Britain and France. Their loyalty would be a concern once the nation went to war in April 1917. In addition, some Irish Americans saw a British defeat as hastening the creation of an independent Ireland. (LC.)

The Tifereth Israel Congregation dedicated the temple on Willson Avenue (East Fifty-Fifth Street) in 1894. Rabbi Abba Hillel Silver took over the Reform-Judaism synagogue in 1917. Until the czar's abdication in 1917, many Jews were generally reluctant to support the Allies because of the pogroms in Russia. Silver and other Zionists looked forward to the creation of Israel after the Allies' victory in the Near East. (CPL.)

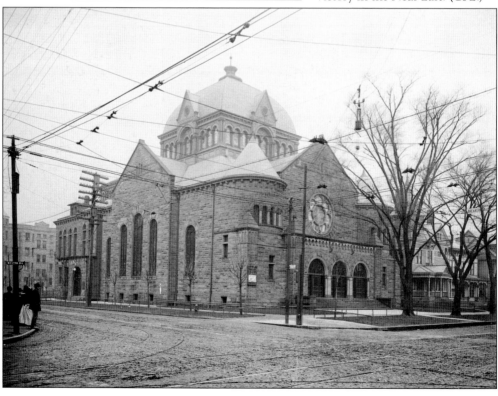

War Secretary Newton D. Baker encouraged the formation of the Jewish Welfare Board to aid Jewish soldiers and sailors in the war. Responsibilities included the recruiting and training of rabbis for military service as chaplains besides overseeing Jewish chapels in the Army and Navy. Among civilian rabbis, Silver gave supplemental support to the board. (LC.)

CIVILIANS

WHEN WE GO
THROUGH THIS
WE NEED ALL THE
HELP AND COMFORT
YOU CAN GIVE.

The JEWISH WELFARE BOARD
United War Work Campaign - Week of November 11·1918

Remember Your First Thrill of
AMERICAN LIBERTY

YOUR DUTY-Buy
United States Government Bonds
2ⁿᵈ Liberty Loan of 1917

The Creel Committee had the task of encouraging immigrants to support the war by purchasing bonds. Cleveland's ethnic neighborhoods included many who had come from Germany and Austria-Hungary. At the same time, their relatives still lived in regions of the Central Powers. Obviously, Czechs, Slovaks, Slovenes, Serbs, Croats, and Poles favored an Allies victory, assuming the result would be independence for their ancestral homelands. (LC.)

Warsazwa became the largest Polish neighborhood in Cleveland because of the employment at the Cleveland Rolling Mills near Broadway Avenue and Jones Road. Immigration peaked in the early 20th century as the Poles fled the repression and poverty of the Polish areas in Germany and Austria-Hungary. Only a small number came from Russia because of restrictions on emigration. (CPL.)

Śladami Ojców Naszych
w Szeregach Armii Polskiej
za Ojczyznę i Wolność

FOLLOWING THE PATHS OF OUR FATHERS IN THE RANKS
OF THE POLISH ARMY FOR MOTHERLAND AND FREEDOM

In the United States, the Polish National Alliance organized to bring about an independent Poland after the war. Working to realize this goal, Poles volunteered to fight with the Polish army in France. The Committee of National Defense represented Polish Americans, who believed an independent Poland was impossible to achieve. Until April 1917, they favored a German victory over Russia to end subjugation in the latter country. (LC.)

N. Y. C. & ST. L. R. R. YARDS

STANDARD OIL CO.

BROADWAY S.E.

Northwest of East Thirty-Fourth Street, Czechs and Slovaks first settled along Broadway before moving south across Kingsbury Run toward Union Avenue. War production made jobs plentiful at Standard Oil and the rail yards. In the background, smoke from the steel mills meant further employment. The Diebolt Brewing Company was another source of work in the neighborhood. (CPL.)

In January 1918, Schauffler Missionary Institution celebrated Founder's Day in a new administration building near Broadway on Fowler Avenue. Mary Wooster Mills, principal of the institution, spoke about Schauffler's Americanization program. Down the block, Fowler School (pictured) offered language classes at night for teaching English to immigrants who had to work during the day. (CPL.)

In May 1915, Helen Zakutna (second row, second from right) graduated from a Slovak Bible school at a Lutheran church in the Tremont area of Cleveland. Her mother immigrated to America in 1888. (See page 56.) Helen later worked at the American Multigraph Company in Cleveland (see page 80), which began producing munitions in 1916. Serving in the US Army, cousin George Zakutna was gassed in the war. (Author's collection.)

The American, Slovak, and Czech flags wave behind a legionnaire fighting in France. The drawing from a recruiting poster written in Czech helped to motivate 350 Clevelanders to join the Czech-Slovak Legion. Those born in Austria-Hungary and not naturalized American citizens were classified as enemy aliens and not eligible to serve in the US military. The enlistees signed up at the recruiting office on Broadway Avenue. Lada Kiml and James Sedlacek won the French Croix de Guerre. (LC.)

Neither Catholic nor Protestant, Czech Freethinkers built Bohemian National Hall at the corner of Broadway and Mead Avenues in 1897. It became the political, social, and cultural center of the Na Vrsku (on the hill) community. Rudolph Friml came to America from Austria-Hungary before World War I. The Czech composer and pianist had studied at the Prague Conservatory under Antonin Dvorak. He settled in Cleveland and taught piano in the Bohemian community. Friml felt at home among his neighbors, many of whom were recent immigrants speaking his native language and favoring an independent Czechoslovakia. After Oscar Hammerstein asked him to write the score for an operetta, Friml made his home in New York City. The theater at Bohemian National Hall would frequently give performances of Friml's many operettas. In October 1915, Czechs, Moravians, and Slovaks met in the hall to organize an alliance dedicated to the establishment of Czechoslovakia. Tomas G. Masaryk, the first president of the new nation after the war, spoke there in 1918. (CPL.)

Workers lowered the level of Mayfield Road for a bridge to accommodate the Cleveland Belt Line Railroad. On the left, Holy Rosary Catholic Church overlooks Little Italy in 1909. Joseph Carabelli, an Italian immigrant, had come to the area in 1880 because of its proximity to Lakeview Cemetery. He founded the Lakeview Marble Works, which attracted stonemasons from Italy. Then, Neapolitans emigrated and toiled in the garment industry. (CPL.)

By the time America went to war, Italy had been fighting the Central Powers for two years. Many Italians returned to their homeland and volunteered for the army and navy. In the poster at left, Fillippo Mezzei (right), a native of Tuscany, fought for the colonies during the American Revolution. A group of 11 residents of Little Italy joined the Lakeside Hospital Unit in 1917, and 1,400 would serve in the American Expeditionary Forces (AEF), with casualties totaling more than 100. (LC.)

"WELCOME Comrade-at-Arms!"

On a Sunday in Cleveland's Buckeye neighborhood, a Hungarian family waits for a streetcar. The number of Hungarians living in the city was second in the nation only to New York. More than 400 Clevelanders served in the Army. The war stimulated the naturalization of immigrants, but most remained aliens. On September 2, 1918, the American Hungarian Federation held a conference in Cleveland and supported Americanization programs. (CPL.)

The Standard Brewing Company of Cleveland made Erin Brew, a beer popular with the Irish. Mostly immigrating before the Civil War, Cleveland's Irish population assimilated into American culture. However, some still identified with the plight of Ireland under the control of Great Britain. They supported Irish rebels fighting for independence with arms from Germany. Under wartime laws, the Justice Department censored Irish American newspapers as being disloyal to an ally. (CPL.)

Charles W. Chesnutt heard disturbing reports of the mistreatment of segregated African Americans in the South's Army camps. He wrote to the secretary of war, whom he had known when Baker served as mayor of Cleveland. Baker asked the generals in charge to investigate the complaints, knowing his actions could not eradicate the evils of racial prejudice. At the same time, Baker believed German propaganda exaggerated most of the complaints. Nevertheless, he sent a memorandum to Emmit J. Scott, former secretary to Booker T. Washington, and asked him to look after the interests of African American soldiers. A reporter for the *Plain Dealer* quotes Baker's comments on the controversy: "I very much regret what seems to be a certain amount of overworked hysteria on the part of some of the complainers, who seem to think that only colored draftees are assigned to duty in service [labor] battalions, whereas thousands of white draftees already have been, and more necessarily will be assigned to duty in such service battalions." (CPL.)

Ironically, the poster portrays African Americans fighting for "Liberty and Freedom" in Europe, while being denied the same rights back home, especially in the South. However, many saw the war as a chance to show they were patriotic and deserving of equal rights. More than 200,000 African American soldiers went to France and mostly worked in service battalions. The racist policies of the US Army led to the conclusion that they were only good for doing manual labor. Under French command, the 93rd Infantry Division (Colored) included National Guard soldiers from Cleveland and other northern cities. Appreciating the respect shown by the people of France, they fought bravely and received many commendations. (Both, LC.)

Seeking jobs and better living conditions, African Americans began the Great Migration out of the South after the nation's entrance into the war. Their population in Cleveland had grown from about 10,000 to almost 35,000 by 1920. Carl Stokes took his oath 47 years later, becoming the first African American mayor of a major US city. In 1968, his brother Louis Stokes won election to the US House of Representatives, the first African American congressman from Ohio. During World War I, their parents left Georgia and came to Cleveland. Charles Stokes, a laundryman, died in 1929. On a cleaning woman's salary, Louise Stokes raised her sons in a public housing project on East Sixty-Ninth Street. Carl and Louis Stokes served in the US Army during World War II and attended college under the GI Bill. They later practiced law together. (Both, CPL.)

Six

ECONOMIC BOOM

Outside in the falling snow, a smiling soldier drinks coffee and eats a piece of pie. He encourages workers on the home front to keep doing their jobs and help win the war. Many patriotic groups assisted them: YMCA, War Camp Community Service, National Catholic War Council, The Salvation Army, Jewish Welfare Board (US Army and Navy), and American Library Association. (LC.)

In this view looking southeast across the Cuyahoga River, industrial pollution darkens the sky over Cleveland. The booming war economy meant more jobs for civilians but also more foul air to breathe. Poison gas on the war front killed many within hours. Air pollution slowly took lives by reducing life expectancy among the city's population. (LC.)

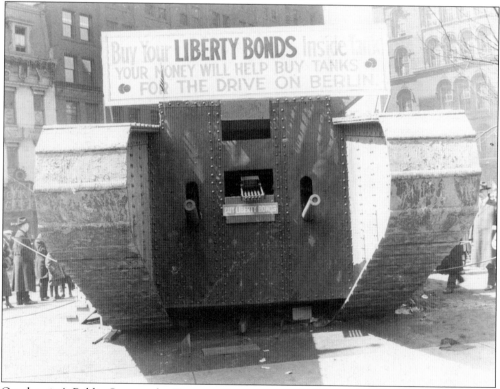

On the city's Public Square, the Treasury Department sold Liberty bonds from inside a heavy tank. American factories made 2,150 heavy and light tanks, but none in Cleveland. However, the armor plate probably came from one of the local steel mills. The Ford Motor Co. in Detroit manufactured light tanks. (CPL.)

In a poster to instill pride among workers, Gen. John J. Pershing congratulates the shipbuilders of America. The US Shipping Board Emergency Fleet Corporation concentrated its efforts on the nation's east coast but did not neglect the importance of shipbuilders on the Great Lakes. Freighters carrying raw materials to lake ports were vital to the steel industry. (LC.)

Pershing Cables:

"The support of the United Army of Shipbuilders at Home is essential to the success of the United Armies at the Front.

"Extend the Army's heartiest congratulations alike to the workmen and management for the splendid results already accomplished by American Shipbuilders."

United States Shipping Board Emergency Fleet Corporation

The Cleveland Ship Building Co., the Ship Owner's Dry Dock Co., and the Globe Iron Works Co. consolidated and formed the American Ship Building Co. in March 1899. The shipyard in Cleveland was located on the west bank of the Cuyahoga River. The booming steel industry increased the demand for ore carriers, especially during the war. (LC.)

A recent migrant from the South works in a shipyard. In August 1918, the *Plain Dealer* reported on Charles E. Hall of the US Labor Department: "Hall has made a tour of Ohio . . . and declared today he has found colored men in large numbers in many skilled trades, helping in the production of war materials, and that colored women are taking a new place in industry." (LC.)

With the assistance of a tugboat, a ship loaded with iron ore steams into Cleveland's harbor. Lake Erie shipping increased dramatically during the war. The *William G. Mather*, the length of a World War I battleship, is preserved as an example of a bulk freighter in the history of commerce on the Great Lakes. The Harbor Heritage Society operates the floating museum on Cleveland's lakefront. (LC.)

George H. Hulett, a Clevelander, invented the ore unloader that bears his name. The Wellman-Seaver-Morgan Co. built Huletts on Whiskey Island in 1912. In one scoop, 17 tons of ore, coal, or limestone could be unloaded from a freighter, decreasing the time to empty the vessel from a week to less than a day. As a result, steel production kept up with the demand of the war economy. (LC.)

Longshoremen load a lake freighter docked in Cleveland. Water and rail transportation moved manufactured goods to markets in other cities. The Warner & Swasey Co. benefited from the demand for machine tools used in war industries. During these years, the business soon became a world leader in the production of turret lathes. (LC.)

C.A. Otis, president of the chamber of commerce, spoke to the Tippecanoe Club at the Hollenden Hotel on January 3, 1918. The *Plain Dealer* reported, "[Otis] emphasized the necessity of coordinating activities of industrial corporations engaged in making war munitions. Maximum production at home he pronounced the greatest need of the nation during the war." (CPL.)

The American Multigraph Company in Cleveland began producing munitions for Great Britain and the United States in 1916. Working day and night, employees made millions of percussion fuses and artillery primers. Among the 1,400 workers were women working for the first time in factories. The plant was located on East Fortieth Street and Kelly Avenue. (CPL.)

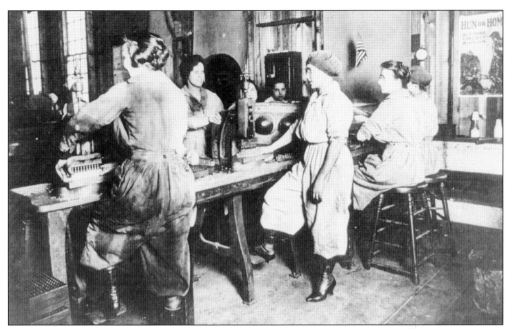

Women load incendiary bullets in an ordnance plant. A poster on the wall tells them to buy Liberty bonds. They received half the wages of men. Usually, females and males used the same restrooms. Working long hours, women and men faced the same risk of developing lung problems from the fumes of the gunpowder. (LC.)

In Lorain, Ohio, women worked for the B&O Railroad, which only employed them because of labor shortages. They did the same work as men but made less money. Doing pick and shovel work, some women maintained the roadbed of the tracks. Unions tended to be unsympathetic to their grievances. In Cleveland, women found jobs as conductors on streetcars to the chagrin of men. (LC.)

The Ohio Woman Suffrage Association opened its Cleveland headquarters on Euclid Avenue in 1912. Three prominent members stand in front of the building: (A) Pres. Bell Sherwin, National League of Woman Voters; (B) Judge Florence E. Allen; (C) Lucia McBride. During the war, the importance of women in the workforce played a role in the 1920 adoption of the Nineteenth Amendment, giving them the right to vote. (LC.)

Teamwork is the theme of this poster that was displayed around the nation. Men and women worked in different jobs producing hats, helmets, boots, putties, tunics, insignias, brushes, rifles, munitions, trucks, ships, trains, airplanes, and foodstuffs. Regardless of their skills, the Lilliputians shared the responsibility of equipping soldiers. No job was too small or insignificant. (LC.)

The White Motor Co. began producing trucks and automobiles on Canal Street in 1906. With the coming of war in 1914, the French government ordered 600 trucks. In 1917, the US Army selected the two-ton White truck as its standard vehicle. By the end of the war, White Motors had produced 18,000 trucks for the United States and the Allies. (CPL.)

The Peerless Motor Car Co. opened a new factory at 9400 Quincy Avenue in 1906. Nine years later, the corporation became a subsidiary of the Peerless Truck and Motor Car Co., which continued to produce luxurious automobiles. During the war, the British bought Peerless trucks and converted them into armored vehicles. (CPL.)

In 1914, Ford Motors built an assembly plant for the Model T at 11610 Euclid Avenue. The declaration of war in 1917 resulted in the curtailment of automobile production for civilians, and the government used the building to store war materials. Ford resumed production in 1919. The US Department of the Interior placed the building in the National Register of Historic Sites in 1976. The Cleveland Institute of Art now owns the structure. (CPL.)

The F.B. Stearns Company was located on the corner of Euclid Avenue and Lakeview Road. The factory produced automobiles and trucks. Stearns won numerous races with his stripped-down cars. During the war years, he made Rolls-Royce engines for airplanes besides Stearns-Knight automobiles. A Toledo firm, Willys-Overland, purchased controlling interest in the company in 1925. (LC.)

Dille Road ran downhill to the steel mills. Most of the laborers took the streetcars on Broadway Avenue. Some lived in the neighborhood or on the hill, and they walked to their jobs in the valley. A good number of them were first- and second-generation immigrants with roots in the war-torn regions of Central, Eastern, and Southern Europe. (CPL.)

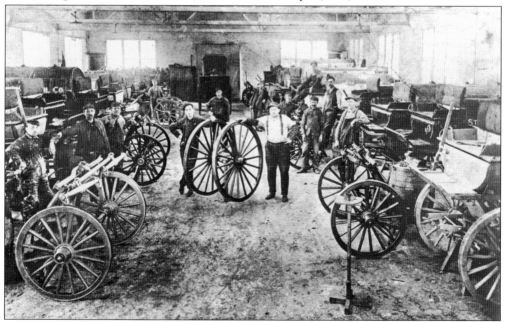

Standard Oil of Ohio built wagons in a factory off Broadway Avenue in Cleveland. John D. Rockefeller and associates founded the Standard Oil Trust, which dominated 90 percent of the refinery industry. The State of Ohio filed a successful suit against the trust in 1892, dissolving it within the state. The US Supreme Court declared the holding company that replaced the trust in violation of federal law in 1911. (CPL.)

By the 1890s, John D. Rockefeller lived most of the year in New York and no longer considered Cleveland his legal residence. He spent the summers in his Forest Hills home overlooking Cleveland and Lake Erie. In July 1917, Rockefeller stayed in the house for the last time. It burned down that December. Throughout the war years, the Rockefeller Foundation gave aid to the suffering civilians in Europe. (CPL.)

In partnership with James Pickhands, Samuel Mather would become the wealthiest man in Ohio. Pickhands Mather & Co. mined and transported iron ore to steel mills. Mather built the most expensive mansion on Euclid Avenue's Millionaires' Row, which survives today on the campus of Cleveland State University. He founded the War Chest and the French government awarded him the Legion of Honor Cross. (CPL.)

Seven

BASEBALL, WORK, OR FIGHT

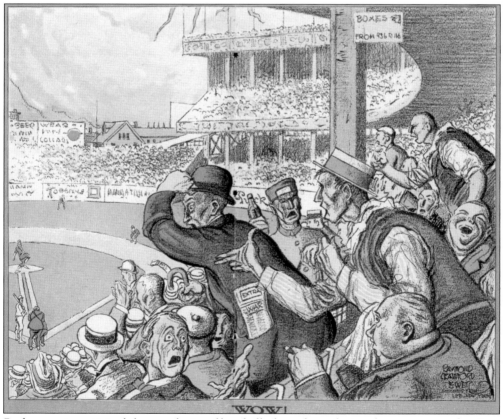

Puck magazine satirized the popularity of baseball, the only professional team sport at the time. The folded newspaper with the phrase "Extra War" in a fan's coat pocket arouses little if any interest compared to the excitement of the game. America's national pastime allowed the fan to either ignore or forget the world's problems—at least until the nation itself went to war. (LC.)

On Sundays, huge crowds watched amateur baseball games at Cleveland's Brookside Stadium, where most of the fans either stood or sat on the surrounding hills. On September 20, 1914, a crowd of 100,000 fans watched the Telling Strollers defeat Hanna's Cleaners for the city championship. Blue laws increased the size of the crowd since the Cleveland Indians could not play on Sundays until 1918. People came to see the game as though it were a social event to attend after church.

The inconvenience of crowded streetcars and the lack of adequate restroom facilities did not seem to be a problem with them. On Saturdays, college football also attracted large crowds on campuses around the nation. The National Football League had yet to be founded in Canton, Ohio, and then would take years to gain popularity. Today, the sport has eclipsed baseball as the favorite among fans. (LC.)

In October 1917, the Treasury Department took advantage of baseball's popularity to sell bonds for financing the war. The first Liberty bond campaign focused on investors from Wall Street, and sales had not gone well. Secretary of the Treasury William G. McAdoo decided to follow the recommendations of his advisers and utilize the nation's obsession with baseball to catch the attention of the average American and small investor. (LC.)

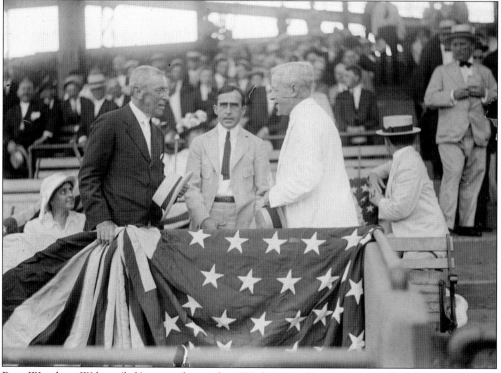

Pres. Woodrow Wilson (left) enjoyed attending Washington Senators games. Besides team owners, fans and players worried about the possibility of a canceled baseball season in 1918. Considering the demands of a wartime economy, Secretary Baker compromised and approved a 140-game season, but the World Series had to start no later than September 5. (LC.)

A news photographer took this picture at a World Series game in 1916. Standing along the railing are, from left to right, Paul and Dorothy Lannin, Bancroft Johnson, and Hanna and John Lannin, owner of the Boston Red Sox. Founder and president of the American League, Johnson liked the chances of the Cleveland Indians winning the pennant in 1918. (LC.)

For some fans, a Puck cartoon lampooned the priority of baseball over the war. Others felt it was only a game and not to be taken seriously. At a time of shortages, baseball was a luxury that wasted resources. Fans riding streetcars to ballparks wasted electricity. Teams taking trains to different cities wasted coal. Critics believed the players should either work in war industries or serve in the military. (LC.)

"DASH IT ALL, THEY'RE PRINTING THE BASE BALL NEWS ON THE TENTH PAGE NOW!"

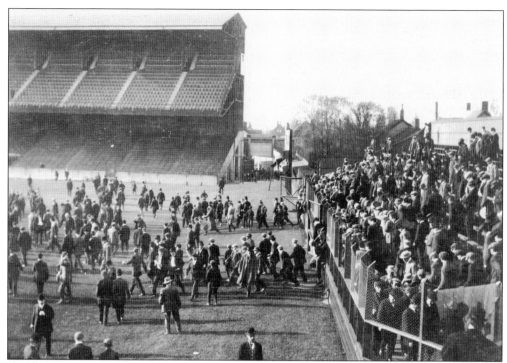

With a capacity of about 27,000 fans, Cleveland's League Park stood at the corner of East Sixty-Sixth Street and Lexington Avenue. Spectators mostly arrived by streetcars. Picnickers could use the field before games. Competing for a pennant all season in 1918, the Indians drew 295,515 spectators, most in the American League. (CPL.)

On Memorial Day 1918, League Park hosted a number of events for the holiday. Cleveland played a doubleheader against Chicago. In between games, Johnny Kilbane and other boxers instructed Army and Navy recruits. Tris Speaker (second from left), star outfielder of the Indians, appears somber, perhaps expecting the season to end at any time. (LC.)

Enlistment and conscription took many players from major-leagues teams, with 775 serving in the military including from the Negro Leagues. Owners had problems fielding talented teams. With players leaving for the military, managers had to draw up different rosters from one game to the next. Attendance declined because fans refused to watch inferior players. (LC.)

"Shoeless" Joe Jackson, a former outfielder for Cleveland, played in only 17 games for the White Sox in 1918. His draft board in Greenville, South Carolina, reclassified him to class one for military service. He claimed exemption as the sole support of his family and worked for a shipbuilding firm in Delaware. Jackson played full-time on the company's team, leading to charges of him being a draft dodger. (CPL.)

On July 19, 1918, word came out of Washington that War Secretary Newton D. Baker, faced with the pessimistic news from France, began to have second thoughts about the status of baseball. A *Plain Dealer* reporter commented, "Baseball must be considered unessential and that the big league season is practically at an end." Baker reconsidered and decided to abide by his original decree on the length of the season. (LC.)

On August 31, 1918, owner James Dunn canceled the last Indians games in St. Louis. In spite of Cleveland sweeping a four-game series with the White Sox in Chicago, Boston had clinched the pennant by two and a half games over the Indians, thanks to the pitching and hitting of Babe Ruth (pictured). The Red Sox went on to defeat the Chicago Cubs in the World Series. (CPL.)

94

Unlike Babe Ruth, Capt. Ty Cobb volunteered to serve in the Army when the shortened season ended. The Indians had swept a doubleheader over the Tigers in Detroit on August 30, 1918. Neither Cobb nor Speaker got a hit that day, perhaps anticipating their upcoming military service. Capt. Cobb served in the Gas and Flame Division and nearly died from poison gas while training in France. (CPL.)

Smoky Joe Wood came down with arm trouble in 1917. Influenza and injuries depleted the Indians early in the regular season of 1918. At the same time, the drafting of players was looming on the horizon. Manager Lee Fohl decided to try out Wood in left field, where he won games with his excellent fielding. Returning to rural New York at the end of the season, Wood harvested crops on his farm. (CPL.)

Terry "Cotton Top" Turner played third base and shortstop for Cleveland from 1904 to 1918. He still holds team records for putouts and games played. Turner had the most stolen bases for an Indians player until Kenny Lofton broke his record in 1996. Turner credited himself with patenting the headfirst base slide. Cleveland's draft board exempted him because of age and health problems. The Indians released Turner on August 25, 1918. (CPL.)

Stan Coveleski grew up in Shamokin, Pennsylvania, a coal-mining town. He played nine years for Cleveland. One of the best spitball pitchers of the era, Coveleski had an excellent season for the Indians in 1918, winning 22 games with a 1.82 earned run average. On May 24, 1918, he pitched a complete game of 19 innings and won 3-2 over the New York Yankees. (CPL.)

In September 1918, League Park stood as an empty reminder of what might have been had the season gone its normal length. The Indians had three lieutenants, three sergeants, a corporal, and two privates in Europe besides seven more former players training in the United States. Owner James Dunn promised to spend money for a championship after the war. (CPL.)

Tris Speaker joined the Navy and attended aviation school at the Massachusetts Institute of Technology in Boston. He now earned $33 a month instead of $2,833. His daily routine included drills, hikes, and calisthenics, in addition to classes on navigation, signaling, and gas engines. However, Armistice Day changed everything. Speaker applied for a discharge and expected to play baseball with the Indians in 1919. (CPL.)

Ray Chapman led the league in runs and walks in 1918. Complying with the "work or fight" policy of the War Department, he joined the Naval Auxiliary Reserve and served until Armistice Day. Chapman improved his hitting in 1919, but again, the Indians finished in second place. He decided to play one more year for friend and manager Tris Speaker. On August 16, 1920, Chapman died from a concussion caused by a pitched ball. (CPL.)

On October 10, 1920, Indians second baseman Bill Wambsganss (pictured) made the first unassisted triple play in World Series history—a record that still stands. Indians outfielder Elmer Smith hit the first grand slam, and his teammate Jim Bagby became the first pitcher to hit a home run in a World Series game. Bagby was the last Indians pitcher to win 30 games in a regular season. Cleveland defeated Brooklyn five games to two. (CPL.)

Eight

BLIZZARD AND INFLUENZA

Under the leadership of Harry Garfield, the US Fuel Administration dealt with the supply and demand for coal in a wartime economy. With the approach of winter in 1917, Garfield wanted to avoid shortages by telling consumers to order coal before the onset of cold temperatures. At the time, accurate long-range weather forecasting did not exist and natural gas heated a minority of homes. (LC.)

A winter storm struck Cleveland on January 12, 1918. The city did not suffer another storm of this magnitude until the Blizzard of 1978. At the same time, the Northeast and Midwest shared the misery of record arctic temperatures and snowdrifts. Coal supplies quickly fell behind demand due to the stoppage of rail traffic. The war was temporarily forgotten as the population battled nature instead of the Central Powers. (CPL.)

Snowfall measured up to 15 inches, with drifts from 10 to 15 feet burying homes and vehicles. The temperature dropped to 15 degrees below zero with winds gusting up to 60 miles per hour. Without coal for home heating, people sought refuge in churches. A change in the weather came in early February as temperatures reached springlike levels. (CPL.)

The health of the child is the power of the nation

APRIL 1918   Children's Year   APRIL 1919
UNITED STATES CHILDREN'S BUREAU AND WOMAN'S COMMITTEE OF THE COUNCIL OF NATIONAL DEFENSE

In April 1918, the Council of National Defense had no idea what health problems lay ahead for the country. On September 22, Surgeon General William Gorgas issued a warning of an impending influenza epidemic. Cleveland delayed taking any action until 12 days later. Director of Public Welfare Lamar T. Beman told Health Commissioner Dr. Harry L. Rockwood to draw up a plan for dealing with the epidemic. (LC.)

Across the nation, the gauze mask became the attire of precaution. A motorman stopped a passenger without a mask from boarding the streetcar. Rockwood ordered motormen of the Cleveland Railway Company to help in the arrest of passengers spitting in streetcars. His plan included the isolation of those with influenza symptoms by suggesting that employers tell sick workers to stay home. (LC.)

PREVENT DISEASE

CARELESS
SPITTING, COUGHING, SNEEZING,
SPREAD INFLUENZA
and TUBERCULOSIS

On October 9, 1918, the *Plain Dealer* published a statement from Dr. Harry L. Rockwood's advisory board about sick residents going to work: "Don't think that by doing so you are helping the country in its war efforts. You may have influenza, spread the disease, and thus deprive the nation of many men's work. It is therefore your patriotic duty to stay at home if you feel indisposed." (NLM.)

Feeling especially vulnerable, mail carriers and other service workers wore masks, which provided no real protection from getting influenza. Health Commissioner Rockwood asked proprietors where the public assembled to bar people with symptoms. He suggested movie theaters show slides on influenza prevention. As the number of cases continued to increase, Rockwood asked city official for stronger measures. (NA.)

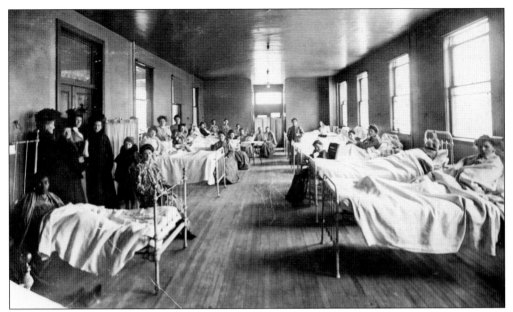

At City Hospital, Health Commissioner Rockwood ordered the isolation of patients with influenza symptoms. The Red Cross gave him $20,000 toward the funding of facilities in the suburbs. For a 10-week period, Rockwood estimated a cost of $122,000 for 1,000 beds and 100 nurses. Claiming the epidemic posed a threat to war industries in the Cleveland area, he asked the Mayor's War Committee for $105,000 to equip an emergency influenza hospital in the city. (NLM.)

At Broadway and McBride Avenues, St. Alexis Hospital served the working-class community starting in 1885. Catholics made up only a quarter of the patients, and three-quarters were charity cases. In 1906, Dr. George W. Crile successfully performed the world's first blood transfusion at the hospital. Along with other hospitals, St. Alexis had an overwhelming number of influenza patients in its wards. At the same time, emergency treatment for industrial accidents complicated matters. (CPL.)

Before the war, Dr. George W. Crile had his office in the Osborn Building at the corner of Prospect and Huron Avenues. The deserted streets in downtown Cleveland illustrate the fear of spreading influenza. Health Commissioner Rockwood ordered businesses to restrict and stagger hours. Offices had to close at 4:30 p.m., retail shops at 5:00 p.m., and department stores at 5:30 p.m. Saloons and restaurants had to lock up no later than 8:00 p.m. (CPL.)

A crowd gathered in the Elysium at Euclid Avenue and East 107th Street. Alarmed at the increase of influenza cases, Rockwood asked Mayor Davis to take more action. As of October 14, 1918, Davis closed schools, theaters, churches, temples, and dance halls. Subjected to complaints from proprietors, he excluded poolrooms, saloons, and cabarets because they did not normally attract large crowds. (CPL.)

Tremont School stood tranquil on Cleveland's Near West Side. Unlike their students, teachers did not have a vacation but instead helped school nurses examining the records of absentees from the previous week. Most of them turned out to be truants, who hoped the schools would remain closed because of low attendance. The board of education considered reopening the schools the following week. However, cases of influenza among the student body increased dramatically, and the classrooms remained closed. (CPL.)

Broadway Methodist Church locked its doors to all worshippers. Health Commissioner Rockwood refused appeals from a number of churches asking to hold services lasting no more than an hour. Police arrested nine men from two Jewish congregations for holding an indoor meeting away from their synagogues. Declaring their innocence, they claimed the gathering was not a religious service but an occasion to worship. (Author's collection.)

On November 2, 1918, four inches of snow fell on Cleveland—the first of the season. A man clears the sidewalk next to the Brooklyn branch of the Cleveland Public Library. Normally, the library would have been open as a place to read or simply to keep warm, but now it remained cold and empty until the lifting of the quarantine. (CPL.)

Many Clevelanders stayed close to home, avoiding crowds and contamination. Charles Chesnutt's house on Lamont Avenue could have been a haven from the influenza if one kept away from the outside world. A teacher in Cleveland, his daughter Dorothy went to work until the schools closed. Nevertheless, she and her sister Helen volunteered to drive nurses to the homes of the sick. (CPL.)

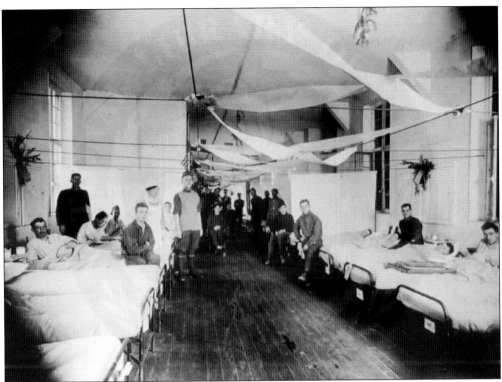

After Armistice Day, soldiers returning from Europe brought more influenza with them. Many perished in the nation's Army camps earlier in 1918. Mobilization led to crowded conditions, causing the rapid spread of the disease. Unfortunately, the government ignored these threats to the nation's health. Former Cleveland Indians player Larry Chappell died in 1918 at an Army base in California. (LC.)

Pres. Woodrow Wilson went to Paris for the Peace Conference after the war. He came down with influenza in early 1919, which kept him from attending important meetings. It also contributed to other physical problems, causing him to suffer a stroke later in the year. The ailing former president poses grimly in 1923, the year he gave his last public address on the radio for Armistice Day. (LC.)

The influenza epidemic caused five months of misery for the residents of Cleveland. From late September 1918 to the end of December, the disease infected 23,644 victims, with almost 1,600 developing pneumonia. More than 3,600 people died from influenza and pneumonia. In January and February 1919, another 800 deaths added to the gruesome total as the epidemic began to wane. Nearly 4 percent of the city's population caught either influenza or pneumonia, and 16 percent died. The death rate of 474 per 100,000 was the worst in Ohio and higher than Chicago and New York City. As many as 675,000 died in the United States, and 43,000 perished in the military. The epidemic accounted for half of the American deaths on the western front. Worldwide, a fifth of the earth's population suffered from the effects of influenza. More died than were lost in World War I, between 20 and 40 million people. (LC.)

Nine

ARMISTICE DAY
AND RED SCARE

Charles E. Ruthenberg, a Cleveland Socialist, opposed American participation in the war. On trial for radical activities in 1920, Ruthenberg told the prosecutor he had converted to Marxism through the Cleveland Public Library. He took out the first volume of Karl Marx's *Capital*. In 1895, Ruthenberg graduated from a Lutheran school, and his mother wanted him to become a minister. (ISRM.)

Charles E. Ruthenberg lived in this apartment at 8111 Madison Avenue in Cleveland, near his birthplace on Florence Street, today's West Eighty-Fifth Street. He married Rose Nickel, and like her husband, she no longer attended church services. While an employee of the Selmar Hess Publishing Company, Ruthenberg organized a debate in the office about the merits of Socialism, which led to management firing him. (Author's collection.)

Puck magazine published this cartoon in 1910, when domestic issues still took priority over foreign affairs: "The trouble with Socialism, my friend, is that it would destroy initiative. Puck is not an advocate of Socialism, but he finds some grime humor in Monopoly's argument against it." The hairy monster may be a caricature of Eugene V. Debs, the perennial Socialist candidate for president and Ruthenberg's mentor. (LC.)

On the Socialist ballot in 1911, Charles E. Ruthenberg ran unsuccessfully for mayor of Cleveland. As a disciple of Tom L. Johnson, Newton D. Barker refused to debate him over the former mayor's policies. All the candidates appeared during a Labor Day rally at Luna Park. Calling for the abolition of Capitalism, Ruthenberg defended the International Ladies Garment Workers, who had been on strike all summer in Cleveland. Baker went on to win the election. (CPL.)

William "Big Bill" Haywood came to Cleveland in 1912 during Ruthenburg's fruitless campaign for governor. As leader of the International Workers of the World (Wobblies), he favored industrial unions over craft unions. At the annual Socialist Party picnic on the grounds of Luna Park, Haywood told the crowd about his hatred of the capitalists, who used violence against strikers. He fled the country rather than go to prison for violating the Espionage Act in 1917. (LC.)

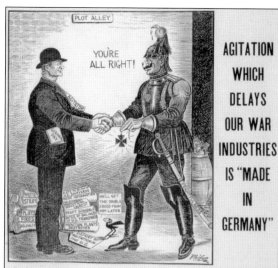

AGITATION WHICH DELAYS OUR WAR INDUSTRIES IS "MADE IN GERMANY"

In the first seven months after America's entrance into this war for human freedom, enemy agitators in our midst caused 283,402 workers to lose 6,285,519 days of production. Our war industries were heavily handicapped by this unpatriotic strife.

LET US ALL PULL TOGETHER TO WIN THE WAR QUICKLY

Name-calling and glittering generalities discredited even legitimate dissent. "Plot Alley" was the scene where the "Agitator" shook hands with the Kaiser. He won the "Iron Cross" besides pocketing "German Pay" for "Disloyalty, Strife, Waste, Fires, and Draft Scandals." All the social and economic problems on the home front were "Made in Germany." Bolsheviks soon replaced the Kaiser as public enemy number one. (LC.)

On May Day 1917, Charles E. Ruthenberg spoke on Cleveland's Public Square, opposing the Conscription Bill, which became law on May 18, 1917. In the coming weeks, Cleveland Socialists continued to criticize the draft until the arrest and trial of Ruthenberg, Alfred Wagenknecht, and Charles Baker. Found guilty of violating the Espionage Act, they spent most of 1918 in the Canton Workhouse. (LCSP.)

Eugene V. Debs gave an antiwar speech near the Canton Workhouse on June 16, 1918. He supported the actions of his three imprisoned comrades and the Bolsheviks, who had taken Russia out of the war. His inevitable arrest for sedition placed him in the same Cleveland courtroom where the same judge decided on the guilt of Ruthenberg, Wagenknecht, and Baker. Judge D.C. Westenhaver found Debs guilty and sentenced him to 10 years in prison. (LC.)

Inside a railroad car in the Forest of Compiègne, the Allies and Germany agreed on an armistice, which would begin at 11:00 a.m. (Paris time) on November 11, 1918. The Treaty of Versailles, signed on June 28, 1919, formally ended the war. Opposed to the League of Nations, the US Senate refused to ratify the treaty. A postcard from the 1930s shows the railroad car in a specially constructed building. (Author's collection.)

Clevelanders celebrated Armistice Day on November 11, 1918. Mayor Harry Davis proclaimed a holiday, leading to the closing of factories and stores. Public Square became the center of the jubilation, with flags waving and people cheering. The festivities continued into the night, including fireworks and more parades. Many intoxicated revelers spent the night in city jails. (CPL.)

In April 1919, soldiers of the 37th Division marched down East Sixth Street to Cleveland's Central Armory. A reporter from the *Plain Dealer* described the scene: "The smiles on the faces of the boys, their hearts warmed by their welcome home, proud smiles on the faces of the wives, sisters, sweethearts, and the mothers to whom the great olive-drab clad throng were just their little boys, grown bigger." (CPL.)

In the postwar years, hopes were high for a better world. Cigars United made this poster for hanging in tobacco shops around the country. However, 1919 turned out to be anything but peaceful. During his presidential campaign the following year, Warren G. Harding said the nation wanted "a return to Normalcy." (LC.)

Strikes occurred in Cleveland and other Ohio cities before the nation entered the war. The Ohio National Guard restored order in Youngstown during a street railway and steel strike in 1916. After Armistice Day, strikes increased as the postwar economy led to worker discontent, often exasperated by the antiunion policies of business. Originally intended as a weapon against German spies and agents, the Espionage Act became the tool to defeat even legitimate grievances. (LC.)

A 1919 political cartoon sums up the thoughts of those who believed strikes resulted from a conspiracy of radicals like the International Workers of the World. William Hayward and 100 other members went on trial in April 1918 for hindering the draft, supporting desertion, and encouraging strikes. After a five-month trial, the court found all of them guilty of sedition. After an unsuccessful appeal, Haywood fled the country and went to Russia. (NA.)

After leaving prison in December 1918, Charles E. Ruthenberg returned to Cleveland, where his left-wing politics contributed to the postwar Red Scare. He organized a parade for May Day 1919. The marchers, many waving red flags, headed for Public Square, where Ruthenberg and others planned to speak. A crowd of opponents blocked the street and a riot ensued. Mounted police restored order but not until hundreds suffered injury and two died. (CPL.)

Journalist John Reed had been in Russia during the Bolshevik Revolution. In March 1919, he came to Cleveland and spoke in Grays Armory. Reed and Ruthenberg were allies in the struggle between the two factions of the radical Socialist Party. Ruthenberg became the first general secretary of the American Communist Party in September 1919. Today, the Kremlin Wall in Moscow still holds the ashes of Reed, Ruthenberg, and Haywood. (LC.)

The United Mine Workers held their convention in Grays Armory on September 9, 1919. Two months later, John L. Lewis, head of the UMW, called a strike against the coal mine owners, who claimed Lenin and Trotsky were behind the labor agitation. Using wartime legislation, Attorney General A. Mitchell Palmer threatened to prosecute him, and Lewis called off the strike. Many miners did not return to work until the union negotiated an agreement. (LC.)

The USS *Buford*, dubbed the "Soviet Ark," transported radical deportees to Finland in January 1920. Congress had passed the Espionage Act of 1917 to deal with the internal threat from Germany. Attorney General A. Mitchell Palmer used the act to round up 249 aliens suspected of being Bolsheviks and anarchists for deportation. Emma Goldman was one of the most notorious of the group. A friend of John Reed, Goldman went to prison for causing a riot in 1893 and then obstructing the draft in 1917. In April 1919, authorities foiled a leftist plot of mailing 36 bombs to business and political leaders, among them John D. Rockefeller and J.P. Morgan. On June 2, 1919, eight bombs exploded in eight cities, including one in front of Palmer's home in Washington. The Justice Department initiated the Palmer Raids to arrest and incarcerate suspected alien radicals. Critics claimed these actions violated the Constitution. The Red Scare had waned by the time Pres. Warren G. Harding commuted Eugene V. Debs's sentence in December 1921. (LC.)

Ten

EPILOGUE—BEREA

The Goethe-Schiller Society of Cleveland erected this statue of Richard Wagner in Edgewater Park. Two years later in 1913, German Wallace College and Baldwin University in Berea merged to form Baldwin-Wallace College, where Dr. Albert Riemenschneider had founded the Conservatory of Music in 1898. Rev. Arthur L. Breslich, a naturalized German American, became the first president of the college. (LC.)

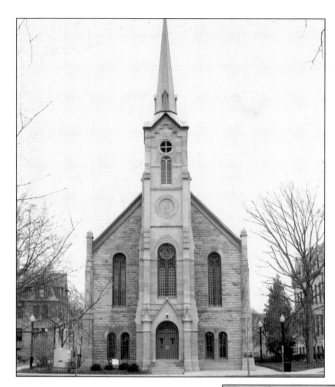

In December 1917, anti-German hysteria gripped the campus of Baldwin-Wallace College. The controversy erupted over the singing of "Stille Nacht" ("Silent Night"), an Austrian Christmas carol. Rev. Arthur L. Breslich had given permission to print copies of the song in German and English for the traditional singing done in the Methodist chapel before Christmas vacation. Students sang it in German and English, while others tore up copies of the song. (Author's collection.)

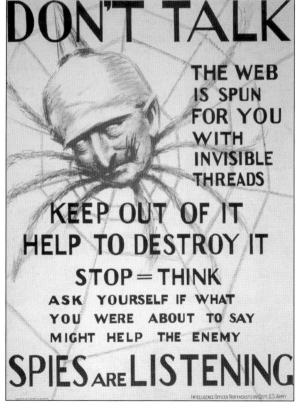

After the outrage over a Christmas carol, businessmen called a meeting, which Breslich attended and denied the charges of being pro-German. Critics circulated a petition signed by the Berea mayor, school superintendent, and other leaders of the community. The petitioners asked the college trustees to take action against all pro-German educators at the college. On January 10, 1918, the trustees reviewed a committee's report and formally removed Breslich from the presidency of the college. (LC.)

Jacob Petschler of German ancestry grew up on Cleveland's West Side and worked as a house painter before entering the Army. In May 1917, the 51st Regiment organized at Chickamauga Park in Georgia and then assigned to the 6th Division in November. The regiment left for France in July 1918. Sergeant Petschler died from wounds while fighting in the Vosges Sector. His grave is in Middleburg Heights' Woodvale Cemetery. (Author's collection.)

Gustav Hausser rose to the rank of sergeant in the 320th Regiment, which had trained at Camp Lee in Virginia. Assigned to the 80th Division, the regiment went to France in June 1918 and fought in the Somme Offensive, along with the Saint-Mihiel and Meuse-Argonne operations. After the war, Hausser attended Baldwin-Wallace College and then taught at West Technical High School in Cleveland. His father was superintendent of the Berea Methodist Orphanage. (Courtesy of Joan Halley.)

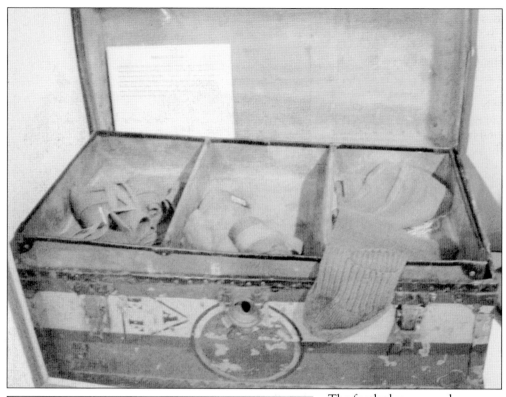

The footlocker, suspenders, puttees, and socks belonged to Lt. Rudolph S. Ursprung. He had enlisted in the Fifth Ohio National Guard and gone to the Mexican border in 1917. After reorganization into the 145th Regiment, Ursprung became a first lieutenant. He suffered a wound in combat and won a Distinguish Service Cross. The French awarded him a Croix de Guerre with a gilt star. (BHS.)

Lt. Corbett Southam served in the Ohio National Guard during the Spanish-American War. On October 13, 1918, Maj. John Southam wrote home to his brother: "It isn't very comforting to see a shell hit a man and toss him 15 or 20 feet into the air and to think the next might have your name and address on it. I hear that Bert Baesel and Joe Brandt have got it." (OHS.)

Two weeks later, the 37th Division joined Belgian and French soldiers fighting in Flanders. After successfully attacking German fortifications, the Buckeyes, on the night of November 2, 1918, crossed the Escault River and firmly established part of its forces on the eastern bank. Two days later, at 2nd Battalion headquarters, Col. Frank Gerlach reported the severe wounding of Maj. John Southam. An artillery shell had fractured both of his legs. (OHS.)

Lidia Southam in Berea knew nothing about the fate of her husband until getting a cablegram at the end of November. He was wounded and in a base hospital. Then the Army reported his death on December 4, 1918. A week later, Major Southam sent her a cablegram saying he expected to undergo an operation soon on his fractured legs. Honorably discharged in 1922 with a 45 percent disability, Colonel Southam was elected mayor of Berea in 1926. (OHS.)

Ralph Caruso's stone marks his grave at the Flanders Field American Cemetery in Waregem, Belgium. He died from the same artillery shell that nearly killed John Southam. In late September, Caruso had saved Southam's life during a gas attack. Also from Berea, Frank Carney and Louis Fritz are buried at the Meuse-Argonne American Cemetery at Romagne, France. (Courtesy of Flanders Field American Cemetery website.)

On September 27, 1918, Lt. Albert Baesel of the 148th Infantry, 37th Division, fought in the Meuse-Argonne Offensive. Hearing the cry of his wounded squad leader, he went to help Cpl. Sterling Ryan, and both died from the bullets of German machine guns. Later, Baesel's men dug a grave and buried him, marking it with a dog tag tied to a cross of broken tree branches. German artillery later destroyed the burial site. (Courtesy of William Stark.)

Four years later, Lydia Baesel received her husband's Congressional Medal of Honor. He finally returned to Berea after a farmer plowing his field unearthed a skeleton with Baesel's dog tag. On April 11, 1926, Mayor John Southam offered a prayer for his late friend at services held in the Conservatory of Music at Baldwin-Wallace College. Afterward, veterans of the 145th Infantry and the regiment's band escorted the caisson bearing the coffin to Woodvale Cemetery. (Author's collection.)

In October 1929, another military service took place in the Conservatory of Music. Mayor Southam had died following an appendectomy. Three generals and five colonels were honorary pallbearers for the 45-year-old war hero. Awarded the Distinguish Service Medal and the French Croix de Guerre, Southam spent five years enduring operations to remove bone splinters from his shattered left leg. His stone is located near Baesel's grave in Woodvale Cemetery. (Author's collection.)

BIBLIOGPRAHY

Briggs, Helen file. Dittrick Medical History Center, Case Western Reserve University.

Chesnutt, Helen M. *Chesnutt, Pioneer of the Color Line*. Chapel Hill: University of North Carolina Press, 1952.

Cleveland in the War. Cleveland, OH: Mayor's Advisory War Committee, 1919.

Cole, Ralph D., and W.C. Howells. *The Thirty-Seventh Division in the World War: 1917–1918*. Columbus, OH: The Thirty-Seventh Division Veterans Association, 1926.

Cramer, C.H. *Newton D. Baker: A Biography*. New York: Garland Publishers, 1979.

Crile, Grace, editor. *George Crile: An Autobiography*. Philadelphia: J.B. Lippincott Co., 1947.

The Encyclopedia of Cleveland History. Website at http://ech.case.edu/index.html

Genealogy files of Albert E. Baesel, Arthur C. Berry, and John R. Southam. Olmsted Historical Society.

Henderson, Frank D., compiler. *The Official Roster of Ohio Soldiers, Sailors and Marines in the World War: 1917–1918*. Columbus, OH: F.J. Heer Printing Co., 1926.

Johnson, Oakley C. *The Day Is Coming: Life and Work of Charles E. Ruthenberg*. New York: International Publishers, 1958.

Johnson, Ray Neil, and Don Palmer. *Heaven, Hell, or Hoboken*. Breinigsville, PA: Kessinger Publishing, 2011.

Longert, Scott H. *The Best They Could Be: How the Cleveland Indians became the Kings of Baseball, 1916–1920*. Washington, DC: Potomac Books, 2013.

Plain Dealer. Cleveland Public Library website at http://cpl.org/newspaper-articles/.

Schaffer, Ronald. *America in the Great War*. New York: Oxford University Press, 1991.

Vourlojianis, George N. *The Cleveland Grays: An Urban Military Company, 1837–1919*. Kent, OH: Kent State University Press, 2002.

ABOUT THE AUTHOR

Dale Thomas is the archivist and former vice president for the Olmsted Historical Society. He lives in North Olmsted, Ohio, with his wife, Lea Thomas, a retired teacher like her husband. They have two sons, Scot and Geoff. Dale is a graduate of Kent State University (bachelor of science in social studies and education) and Case Western Reserve University (master of arts in history). In addition to serving as a judge for History Day at Case Western Reserve University, he has been an adviser for tours at the Western Reserve Historical Society, historian for the Cleveland Civil War Roundtable, and a member of the North Olmsted Landmarks Commission. He is the author of four books: Images of America: *North Olmsted* and Then & Now: *Olmsted* (Arcadia Publishing, 2008 and 2011); *Lincoln's Old Friends of Menard County Illinois* and *Civil War Soldiers of Greater Cleveland: Letters Home to Cuyahoga County* (History Press, 2012 and 2013). (Author's collection.)

DISCOVER THOUSANDS OF LOCAL HISTORY BOOKS FEATURING MILLIONS OF VINTAGE IMAGES

Arcadia Publishing, the leading local history publisher in the United States, is committed to making history accessible and meaningful through publishing books that celebrate and preserve the heritage of America's people and places.

Find more books like this at
www.arcadiapublishing.com

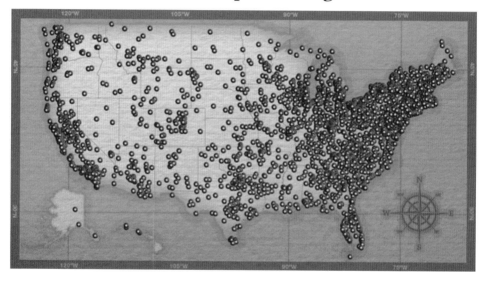

Search for your hometown history, your old stomping grounds, and even your favorite sports team.

Consistent with our mission to preserve history on a local level, this book was printed in South Carolina on American-made paper and manufactured entirely in the United States. Products carrying the accredited Forest Stewardship Council (FSC) label are printed on 100 percent FSC-certified paper.

MADE IN THE
USA